Reaching Higher Heights

By

Lydia M. Douglas

P.O. Box 2535
Florissant, Mo 63033

Copyright ©2007 by Lydia M. Douglas

All rights reserved. No part of this book may be reproduced or transmitted in any form by any means, electronic, mechanical, photocopy, recording or otherwise, without the consent of the publisher or the author, except as provided by USA copyright law.

Cover Designed by Sheldon Mitchell of Majaluk

Manufactured in the United States of America

Library of Congress Control Number:

```
ISBN 13:     978-0-9816483-0-9
ISBN 10:     0-9816483-0-4
LCC Number:  2008924570
```

All scriptures are taken from the King James Version of the Bible.

For information regarding discounts for bulk purchases, please contact Prioritybooks Publications at 1-314-741-6789 or rosbeav03@yahoo.com. You can contact the author at ldoug48305@aol.com.

Reaching Higher Heights

By

Lydia M. Douglas

PriorityBooks Publications
Florissant, Missouri

Table Of Contents

Acknowledgments	i
Dedication	iii
Introduction	1
Dress for Success	2
Savings Plan	4
Saving a Dime	6
The New You	7
The Gift Of life	10
Enthusiasm	11
Rise Above Stereotypes	15
Don't	18
Wounded but Healed	19
Why Not Be Unrealistic?	22
Helping To Rebuild Character in Our Young People	24
Character Building	27
Enemies of Life	30
Mount Up	33
Life with a Purpose	34

The Cracked Pot	36
Finding Your Special Place	39
Lessons Learned	43
Creating the Audacity of Hope	45
It's School Time Again	48
Life Can Be Challenging	54
Summer Challenge Part II	56
Turning Stress into Success	58
Attitude	61
Something to Think About	63
Learning Has Purpose	64
Every Success Starts With a Plan	66
Intellectual Growth	68
Food For Thought	70
Tips for Becoming Successful	73
Notes	77
About the Author	86

Reaching Higher Heights

Acknowledgments

First, I would like to give thanks to all of the young people who have heard and received the positive messages I have been relaying. And of course the teachers who thought I was worthy enough to stand before their classes and conduct my presentations.

I thank all of the business owners, school administrators, youth group leaders and church officials who have allowed me to conduct presentations for students and parents alike.

I thank my neighbors, friends and church members who have shown a great interest in my continuing to reach our young people. I thank all of you for your encouraging words.

I thank my mother, Mrs. Willie V. Savage-Coleman, and step-father, Mr. Nathan Coleman for their loving support.

To the students who have taken the time to write me letters. Indeed, it makes me feel great to know that you are being touched by my words.

I would like to thank Charlotte Petty, editor of the Spanish Lake Word Newspaper for allowing me to share my message in her newspaper.

To my publisher, Rose Jackson-Beavers, who has shown her support and encouragement for me to continue my writings in support of teenagers and the barriers they must overcome.

To my adult friends who say they need encouragement, as well. Thank you for your votes of confidence.

Thanks again to the students who request that I come back again and again to their classrooms to conduct presentations.

To everyone who chooses to read the contents of this book, I thank you for your time. Be sure to pass on the knowledge that you gain to our young people.

Dedication

This book is dedicated to James H. Douglas, Sr., my husband of thirty-nine years. James passed away on September 30, 2007. He was my biggest supporter, no matter where I went he was there supporting me. He was truly my best friend, husband, and a great father to our three sons, Gerry (Angela), Mark (Michelle), James Jr. (Stacye). He was also a very supportive and loving grandfather.

Introduction

Adolescence is an extremely challenging and chaotic period of time. I am a witness to this, since I once was a teenager myself. I may not be where you are now, but I once was a confused, moody, curious teen. My main objective in writing this book is to provide you with a set of strategies that will hopefully encourage and motivate you to strive for and achieve a heightened level of success in both school and work.

Always remember that no dream is out of reach. Education is the key that will unlock any door you choose to walk through. I believe in you! But it is up to you to map out your goals, develop a strategy to achieve them and then forge ahead with as much effort, sacrificing and self-confidence as is needed to be the best you can be.

Most importantly, don't allow any negative forces to block your path. Whenever you begin to feel like quitting, remember these words spoken by Michael Jordan, "Obstacles don't have to stop you. If you run into a wall, don't turn around and give up. Figure out how to climb it, go through it, or work around it."

Dress for Success

With the changing times and fashions, some things should not change. We should never change our values and morals based on what the world or others have decided we should do. You do not need validation or confirmation from anyone.

We need to always remember who we are, no matter what everyone else is doing or saying. Just remember you are an individual, with your own self-esteem. So with all of that said, when you go for an interview, dress for success. Because when the opportunity arrives, you will be representing yourself and no one else.

Remember the company you are applying for will look at you as one who will represent their company and they want to be represented well. So be very careful as to how you represent and carry yourself. There is an old saying that holds true today: "First impressions are lasting impressions." Therefore, if you start dressing with that in mind now, it will become a natural part of your dress and self-esteem.

Your self-worth is based on more than just your outward appearance. Your morals and values will be seen through the eyes of others by the way you carry yourself and that tends to coincide with the way you dress. It is also important to maintain a nice, polite attitude, along with a well-rounded vocabulary and some knowledge of the company you are applying to with hopes of starting a career.

Allow yourself to learn something about the company you wish to work for. That way you will have some input into the interview conversation. Life tends to respond to our outlook, so you need to shape your life to meet the expectations. Do not join easy crowds, because you will not grow. Allow yourself to go in a direction where the demands are high and your performances are even higher.

Tips for Successful Interview Attire

- Do not wear tight clothing.
- Make sure clothes fit properly
- Wear a color that suits your skin complexion. Dark blue and black are still great interviewing colors.
- Refrain from being too stylistic. You can do that on your own time.
- Females should wear a jacket and skirt or a suit. A dress is fine, too. No cleavage should show and the dress or skirt should be either at the knee or below.
- Males should wear a white shirt and dark slacks. However, as long as the shirt is wrinkle free and has sleeves that is fine. A neck tie would be impressive, but people understand if a teenager comes to an interview without one.

Savings Plan

Once you get a job you should immediately begin a savings plan, if you don't have one already. A plan can start with you recording how much you spend from Monday through Sunday on shopping, eating out, and going to movies. You will be surprised at the amount you spend. Oh, don't forget the cell phone.

Many teens have succumbed to the cell phone craze, spending thousands of dollars on using their cell phones during peak times. If you put the money you are paying on your cell phone bills into a savings account, you would be surprised to see the amount of money you may accumulate. If you start now with just a small amount you will be amazed at how fast it will grow. Even saving pocket change will add up. A few dollars will turn into a few more before you know it. And even more if you put forth greater effort.

Saving money not only helps you, but can help your parents or other family members, as well. Think of the things they could use the money for. The more you save the more your family can save. In doing this, you will be learning life lessons that will stay with you forever. You have to have some discipline in order to handle your finances. Wasting money on things that you cannot see will get you nowhere in the long run. I challenge you to develop a savings plan that works for you and put it into action.

The Following Tips May Help You Save Several Hundred Dollars A Year:

- Purchase a bank or large container and drop all loose change in it. Do this daily.
- If you must have a cell phone, live within the plan. Refrain from making calls during peak time, unless it is an emergency. Let your friends know not to call you until your off-peak minutes kick in.
- Buy bargains. Shop at discount stores and watch the amount you save. Fashions come and go, so don't spend so much money on something that will not be popular in the next few months.
- Put at least five to ten percent of your net pay into your savings account.

Saving a Dime

There is nothing wrong with saving a dime,
It's far better than doing hard time for a crime.
Save your money each week if you can,
It's the only way you really can depend,
On yourself and your skills, this should be your basic plan,
Learning to save for the future, is the best advice I can give,
It will help you get to the next step in the life you want to live.

RM Jackson

The New You

We all have newness about ourselves. We have to reinvent ourselves constantly. There are times in our lives when we do not make the best decisions and we make wrong choices that hurt.

Luckily, we only have to live with bad choices for a moment, until the light of life shines on us once again. Once we change our direction to a more positive one, there emerges a new person and the old person is no longer around. We all have gone through times in our lives when we were obviously alive and breathing, but not living. We were not living because we walked around like the dead, alone and not making any decisions. But not anymore.

A new life comes from being broken sometimes. In many instances, trials come to make us stronger. With every trial there is always another way to look at it. Ask yourself, what can I learn from all of this? Was it an error in judgment on my part that caused it or was it something or someone else?

There is a lesson to be learned and when you get to the other side of the situation you are able to learn a valuable lesson. You have always wanted to just live a normal life; well, here is the new normal. When the new you is formed, that is the time to clean up or take inventory of your mind. We find ourselves cleaning out closets and discarding old stuff we no longer need, but what about the closets in our minds? We forget that when our minds become cluttered, we need to release the junk that threatens to set us off track. Carrying around these bags of garbage in our minds causes many problems, like stress and becoming overloaded with sicknesses. Being stressed out hurts your body in many unhealthy ways, so let the clutter go.

Since our destiny is shaped by our thoughts and actions, it is important to keep our minds free of clutter. Change negative thinking into positive thoughts. Forget the woes of yesterday and look toward tomorrow for greater joy. You have the ability to change every broken aspect of your life.

Celebrate the new you!

You can do anything with your life, because it belongs to you. You can turn nothing into something. You can conquer all of the negativity in your life and turn it into positive, and you don't need anyone's validation to do it. With the rapid changes in this world, we have to keep re-evaluating ourselves in order to keep up with the changes. Continually ask yourself, "Am I going to view life from the sidelines or become a key player in the game called life?"

Think about it. In the life of sports most players do not want to be a bench warmer. That's how it is in our lives, too. We should want to have major roles in who we are to become. Say to yourself, "I am taking charge of my life from now on. The old things have passed away, behold all things are made new. I will do a new thing and it will come forth." The Bible discusses this very issue in Isaiah 43:19.

Focus on the words of Maya Angelou: "I can be changed by what happens to me, but I refuse to be reduced by it." Think of these words as you celebrate the new you. Be open enough to discover new things about yourself, and please do not sell out your virtue and values for something you think you want in life. Always decide what's right before you decide what's possible.

Ralph Waldo Emerson said, "What lies behind us and what lies before us are small matters compared to what lies within us." Don't let stumbling blocks prevent you from becoming what you can become. Stumbling blocks are too easy to be removed.

Now that you are in touch with your past and understand the present, you can now move toward your future. Remember these words as spoken by Muhammad Ali: "The man who has no imagination has no wings." What strong words. Saying these words out loud should make you look deep inside yourself to pull up all the abilities and strengths you will need to celebrate your life and dreams.

The Gift Of life

The Gift of Life is something to behold
From our ancestors it's a great story to be told
From our past to our present
Our journey was tough
But it made us stronger and our minds robust
There is a purpose in this life for each of us
Don't sell yourself short, just believe and trust
This gift of life was given to you, so start celebrating
It's all about you!

Rose Jackson-Beavers

Enthusiasm

Webster's Dictionary describes enthusiasm as a passionate zeal for something or someone. What are you passionate about? Are you enthusiastic about the life you are living or preparing yourself for? If we don't get excited about something in life, maybe we need to review our surroundings. Fear is not an option. Why? Because your goals should be work to become, not just work because. When people work to become they tend to set their goals high. If you are working just because, you tend to walk around with a cluttered and unhappy mind.

It is important to get excited. This will bring your enthusiasm to the next level. This will give you personal power and that power will give you two areas you can work from to increase your power. They are:

1. Taking responsibility: It is all about you, so you have to take responsibility for your choices and your actions.
2. Taking action: When you take the best action, you will get the best result.

All this is for you to realize that your life belongs to you and you alone. If you don't get excited about it, then no one else will. Only you have the power to allow your spirit to soar.

You must develop a zeal for something and then put all of your effort toward bringing it to pass. Remember that this is your life. The choices you make will affect you first. So why not get excited and unleash the genius inside you.

There are many doors already open, and the crowns have already been fought for and are laying in wait for you to pick them up. We are standing on the shoulders of some great leaders and we are not going to allow their hard work to be in vain. Let their lives give you the light to see your way.

Keep your associations with people who are setting positive goals in their lives. Find others who are enthusiastic about life just as you are. Their life will impact your life just as yours will impact theirs. You will be able to help and encourage each other. This will be a win-win situation.

For every successful person there is someone behind them, pushing and encouraging them. No one succeeds alone. Allow the ideals of others to lift your spirit to your highest potential. When you make good, positive decisions they will be with you for the rest of your life.

Why not be enthused about it? When you share with others, no matter what it is, one thing is for sure, what leaves one heart will find the heart of others.

If you see the person you want to be, with hard work and persistence, that's the person you will be. By far, the person others see on the outside should be the person you are on the inside.

You cannot give happiness without feeling it yourself. Others will see the joy and excitement when you are true to yourself. Create a friendly atmosphere on the inside and it will show on the outside. You have to like yourself before anyone else can.

If you continue to create a positive feeling the new ideas will continue to take place in your mind and heart. One important thing to remember is to prioritize your desires and dreams. Once again, this is your life. Read about other people's successes and failures. Learn from them. There is always a lesson to be learned before you hit that brick wall.

The more reasons you can come up with for making you happy, the more happiness you will encounter. You only reap what you sow. You can turn all of your dreams and visions into reality. Now that's true excitement.

The point of this message is just to be happy and to help make this world a much happier place to live. At the end of the day you will be able to relax and say, "Well done, I did something worthwhile today." Do not allow negativity to describe you. After all, you only have one life to live, why not take the challenge to succeed and be happy?

There is a great difference between earning a living and living your life. You can do both and be happy with your choices. As long as you are emotional about your choice then you will be able to put forth all of your best efforts. From this you will be excited, happy, and your enthusiasm will show.

Dr. Martin Luther King said it best. "The ultimate measure of a man is not where he stands in moments of comfort and convenience, but where he stands at times of challenge and controversy." Occasionally in life there are those moments when we feel totally fulfilled, when this happens we should reflect on this and seek to feel this way all the time.

Rise Above Stereotypes

There are stereotypes hanging over certain ethnic and religious groups. We are sometimes stereotyped by the neighborhood we live in, our gender or race, and the friends we associate with. We are tied into a lump that all people of a certain race eat the same type of food or like the same things. This is not true for all individuals. We are all created differently to fulfill different tasks in life. No matter what some people may say, we are our own person.

If you are told you are not going to college or that you will not be anything in life, don't believe it. This does not apply to everyone. You can be whatever or whomever you want to be. You can rise above stereotypical views. There is a door that stands open with your name on it. All you have to believe is that you can walk right through it. Then just do it. Education is the key that will unlock that door. Finish your education and be everything successful you hope to be.

We are not the same. What is good for one person may not be good for the next one. A good example of this is the fact that most people think all African-Americans eat sweet potato pie and pigs' feet. Even though I am an African-American, I do not eat sweet potato pie or pigs' feet. So, my point is, do not allow another person's label to become attached to you. You have choices. If you want to go to college, go ahead, become a doctor, nurse, attorney, executive, or whatever. You can do it. Go for it. Do not listen or play into anything negative. Negativity is a joy stealer.

Do not play into all of the preconceived notions about what others do not know about you. You do not owe anyone any explanations for yourself or your actions. Just do whatever you want to do and it will show all by itself.

Knowledge is power. That's your tool to break all preconceived notions of who you are, where you are to end up, or what you are going to become. Allow your success to speak for itself. Look fear right in the face and tell yourself that you will succeed in whatever area you so desire.

Know who you are without a shadow of a doubt. Stand up and face the world, and declare you will succeed and become all that you want to become. Just tell yourself, "I will arise and be all I want to be."

Understand your personal mission. Do not be sidetracked by others' misconceptions. You must be clear about your own destination. You are not bound to live your life according to others' opinions of you. The best weapons against stereotypes are knowledge and education.

I have discovered that I do have choices and sometimes all it takes is a change in my attitude. Do not look down on another person. We can always learn from others, but do not allow anyone to label you in any way. Our lives begin to end the day we become silent about the things that matter to us. No one else can tell you how to live your life. You have to make that choice yourself. Do not allow anyone to take that choice away from you.

As Oprah Winfrey said, "Your belief in yourself can move you forward or you can allow the opinion of others to hold you back." I say, the choice is yours.

Don't

Don't sit here and dream to be a King or Queen
Get up, reach high and change your negative routines
Don't say okay, just to get by another day
Change your life and impress yourself
Today, tomorrow and always.
Success can happen if you work real hard,
Graduate, work, progress and get a better job.

Rose Jackson-Beavers

Wounded but Healed

How many people do we meet on a daily basis who are wounded? How much hurt do we pass each day? How many times do we put on our church face? People are wounded and hide their pain behind a mask of deception. Some people are in pain because they feel they don't have any choices and when you feel this way, you can easily lose your way.

I have discovered that I do have choices. I myself have been wounded, but now I am healed. In the healing process I decided that I was not going to remain on the level that I was on. I saw many good things in life and I wanted to take advantage of some of them for myself.

One of my favorite scriptures states, "There were empty spaces and broken pieces, but I managed to put them all back together again. My spirit person had to be healed in order for me to see through the clouds in my life. A potter runs a potter's wheel, I knew the Potter and I was the clay, I asked to be put back on the wheel until I was mended again. That's when all of the pieces started to come together." Jeremiah 18: 2-4. KJV

That's the way I felt until I made a choice to go back to school. It was hard to work 8-10 hours a day and go to school at night, but I did it. I realized that my goals and visions had not dissipated or dissolved. They were still there, in the pit of my heart.

I had been wounded by the choices I had made. At that time, I did not know that my choices had consequences. But through it all I did not allow my choices and errors in judgment to dominate my life. I made up my mind that I was going forth with my life. I figured out what I wanted to do and began to work on it. I realized what my values were and the fact that I am worth more than any error gone badly in my life. I turned off the rewind button and hit start again.

I learned from my mistakes and focused on my strength. That was when I found the courage to try again. I realized that we do have choices and all we need to do is change our attitude about where we are. Being successful in life has to start with you first. With a made up mind, that's the first step to becoming successful in life.

The Healing Has Begun.

Our destiny was shaped the day we were born. Even though we get off track sometimes, that does not mean we cannot get back on track and start again. We cannot allow the judgment of others to stop us from accomplishing anything we want to do. We can make changes in our lives, all we have to do is be relentless and never give up.

Even though you might have been wounded, you can be healed. Take the first step in faith, even though you might not see the last step of the journey, just step out anyway. With faith, nothing is impossible. If you have faith in what you want to do and it comes to pass, then no explanation is necessary. Make sure you are on the path for you and not for someone else. You have to live your life for you, and once you do this, your happiness for life will come. Now that unstoppable courage and zest for life will be on the horizon.

I had many goals in my life and I knew they were attainable. I had an unstoppable wave of energy within and with persistence my goals and dreams have matured into a reality. I also felt fearful, but I told myself, "I am going to make my dreams come true, no matter how long it takes." And they all have come true. The only time I look back is to share my testimony with others and to let them know that if I can move forward without regrets, then so can they.

It is a faith journey. You have to believe in the powers that be. On my journey I did not have anyone to talk to about how I felt. I found God along the way. I already knew of Him, but I found Him in the midst of my hurt. If you are reading this, this is just one of my dreams that have come true.

When I hear the words of Maya Angelou's poem, *Still I Rise*, I shudder because they touch my soul. "You may write me down in history with your bitter twisted lies, you may trod me in the very dirt, but still I rise…" Now those are words that should give you the strength to achieve all you can.

Why Not Be Unrealistic?

Why not go out on a limb? When the fruit harvesters harvest their fruit they go to the limb of the tree, because that's where the fruit is. So why not go out on a limb to be what you want to be? Don't allow others to convince you that your ideas are crazy and unrealistic.

Let's stop and think for a while. Was it realistic for the person who came up with the idea of a computer, microwave oven, remote control, automatic dishwasher, and washer and dryer?

Was it unrealistic a few years ago that e-mail would someday take over the post office? Was it unrealistic to believe that we could pay our bills on the Internet? You can now even e-mail your local post office and they will come to you and pick up your packages.

All of these things began as ideas in the minds of other people. But look at all the ideas now. All of them have been accomplished. How was all of this possible? These people did not give up or allow others to tell them they could not do what they were thinking about doing. They took the necessary steps to bring their ideas to the table. Now what about the goals you have set for yourself? As far as the idea you thought was crazy or ridiculous, this should give you the courage to go out on that limb, reach up and out and get whatever you want out of life.

Just think for a while, you would not have the idea if you

could not come up with the plan and details to put it all together. You will not be challenged beyond your ability to make it work. Just know that you have a huge reservoir of resources within you to do whatever you want to do.

Be ready for setbacks and roadblocks that will possibly get in your way. With a positive attitude you can do anything you want to do. Remember, the idea started with you. You know all the details. Even though sometimes you might have to seek the help of others to bring it to reality, just know you can.

Others will not see your dream the same way you see it, but do not get discouraged or quit. Even though it might take a while to accomplish certain tasks, do not give up. Instead, get excited about the possibilities. You have to be committed through the good times and the bad. Perhaps your excitement and commitment will influence others.

Helping To Rebuild Character in Our Young People

A person with character does not put a lot of emphasis on the things of life, but on life itself. As far as our young people are concerned, without having established their character they will not know the difference between being alive and living. Our goal and mission should be to help them see their character in everything they do and say.

We need to help our young people make their lives a masterpiece for themselves first, and then others will see the work of art that exists within them. We need to show our youth that we do care about them. The family structure has been broken so badly, that I feel we as adults have a tremendous task before us in reaching our young people.

Life without love is like a flower that has not bloomed due to improper care. It has no beauty or fragrance to share. This is the same way it is with children, they bloom with love and care. We have to show them that they do have something positive to share. Their past is behind them and now they can look toward the future with their heads up and make it whatever they want it to be.

We have to let them know that their choices do have consequences and they themselves are accountable for the outcome. Adults have a great responsibility in encouraging them to continue on. They too have dreams and goals, as well. Even though there has been a slight interruption in fulfilling their dreams, remind them that no condition is permanent. They can pick up the pieces of their lives and move on.

So many leaders have walked before us and we should follow their patterns. We should reach back and help the next generation to become great leaders, as well. We need to let them know that nothing is impossible, if they want to get their lives back on track and fulfill their dreams.

Such a high number of our youth need a new direction or path in life and we cannot afford to allow them to slip through the system. Lots of times we fail to understand what it is they are saying and that breeds mistrust. They just need a little bit of our time. I have found that sometimes a hug will do. They just need a reminder that they should not allow anything to dim the light that shines from within.

Be honest with teens when they ask questions. When they ask if I have ever been a drinker or smoker, I tell them, I used to drink and even tried to smoke, but then I realized that neither one of those things were good for me and I stopped. Then I tell them the dangers involved with abusing these vices.

I tell them that I did not want to be known by my container, but by my contents. Not by the cigarette or drink in my hand, but by what's on the inside of me.

I can laugh as loud as anyone else with a bottle of water or diet soda in my hand.

In that way, I am connecting with them somewhat. I am not putting myself on top and looking down at them. Sometimes, I will put my arms around them and to my surprise their eyes fill up with water and smiles come forth. I told one young man that if he kept smoking, by the time he gets my age his lungs will be in bad shape. He put his cigarette down. I told him I tried smoking but could never inhale, so I stopped trying. Another one I told, "I can laugh just as loud at a party or gathering as anyone else with a bottle of water in my hand or nothing at all. I do not have to drink just because it is there."

I am always asking, "Where do you go to school?" Once I get them to talk about education I encourage them to continue on. All of this will help build or re-build character in our young people. With just a little bit of encouragement their self-esteem will go to the next level.

"The ultimate test of a man's conscience may be his willingness to sacrifice something today for future generations whose words of thanks will not be heard."

Gaylord Nelson

Character Building

How do you rate your character? Is your character your bond? Can others rely on your word? Well, all of this and much more is what character building is all about?

Once you commit to doing something, can others feel with confidence that you will come through? If not, do you let someone know as soon as possible that you can't fulfill their request? If our character is in tact, then we will follow up with a phone call, e-mail, visit, or whatever type of communication necessary. Our word says a lot about us, as far as our character is concerned.

Keep telling yourself, "My self-worth is on the line here, and long after I have parted company, I want my self-worth to remain standing." Whatever others think of me will remain in their minds for sometime to come." Do not leave them with anything negative.

Many times we agree on issues while our emotions are at peak level. When the excitement is over, will your word stand the test of time? Allow yourself to have courage and confidence in everything you say or do. Life will always be just what you make it. So when you make a decision on anything keep in mind that your overall appearance is not just in what you have on or what you say, it's where you stand in your goals and deeds.

If that's an area where you feel weak, then now is the time to make some important changes in your life. Just be patient and all things will come to pass. If you truly want or desire to make a change in your life you can. Always allow the person on the inside to be the person others see on the outside. You are now on your way to living a very enriched and fulfilled life.

Character building does not happen overnight. If changes need to be made, then the first step is to recognize and admit where the weakness is. Many times when we are in need of making changes in our lives, we often look in the wrong direction or area.

Sometimes we can't see our faults for looking in another direction, or listening to others. Sometimes the opinions of others will either raise or lower our self-esteem. It's never a good idea to hang around negativity. It is the biggest joy-stealer that can come along. Go deep within your inner being and find the good buried there and bring it out. That is character building.

Making a decision to change your character has a lot to do with who or what you become in life. Character building involves moving away from past mistakes and errors that have been made along the way. Your character is in your hands and heart. You will count no day lost in which you did all you could do to make a change in your life.

Think about this, can you see your character being fashioned? Look at your actions, your words and thoughts. Are they moving toward a good person of character? Your philosophy of life is best expressed in the deeds and the life you leave behind.

Enemies of Life

Lack of courage in one's life is largely due to past experiences or the will to try. Since we reap what we sow, we need to keep two words in mind:

Shrink and Expand.

These definitions are from Webster's Dictionary.

Shrink—to contract, to dwindle, or to draw back. When we lose sight of what we want to accomplish in life, our dreams and self-esteem have a way of shrinking. With each day we put forth less effort than the day before.

Expand—to spread out, to enlarge, to increase in volume or bulk. Staying focused on your dreams will get you where you want to be in life. You will be able to take your goals to the next level. You might have to implement some changes along the way, but that's okay. These changes are for you.

These words are called "Enemies of Life." If we allow the enemy to take over we will not be able to go forth or move from one point to another. The enemies of life will steal your joy, your dreams, your motivation for all the things you ever thought about doing.

The way to conquer the enemy is to tell yourself, "I have goals to pursue and dreams to accomplish." If you don't take charge of your own life, all of the courage you once had will diminish a little bit at a time.

No matter what your dreams are, they will be lost without courage to forge ahead. With courage comes faith. Faith is taking the first step even when you don't see the end result. Don't allow anything to rob you of your courage, faith or self-determination.

You might run into a couple of problems along the way, but you don't have to allow it to put you in a downward position. You will not be where you want to be overnight, but with each passing day you will be one day closer to your desired goal.

Always remember that when night comes, it's the end of that day and when morning comes it's a new day, so all that did not get done on yesterday will be emerged into the new day. The point is, do not put off for tomorrow what you can do today. Make each day count. Once the day is gone it is gone forever.

No one but you can limit your growth. Just be patient with yourself. Heroes are not made overnight. A hero is an ordinary individual who finds the strength to persevere and endure, in spite of overwhelming obstacles. And when they come, rely on your faith, strength and courage to see you through.

Sometimes life seems so hard you will be afraid to look back and afraid to move forward. During these times just look deep within yourself and you will see the one person who really believes in you, the one person who knows the real you. That person is you.

Not everything you will face can be changed, but nothing can or will be changed until it is faced. Sometimes we are told things like, "You are not going to make it in life." That is a real joy stealer. That's another enemy of life we sometimes have to wrestle with. If you give in to negativity, that's when your life will begin to end.

Just give life another chance, and another, and another, however many it takes. The person who fears failure is limiting him or herself by being afraid to try anything new. One's future is being purchased daily by what is being invested in it. Always follow through with your passion for life. Do not allow the enemies of life to steal your joy.

Mount Up

Mount up to fly as high as you can
Remember you are as big as your dreams
Adeesha Beavers

Life with a Purpose

As children begin to grow, there is a great need to make sure there are some values planted in the soil of their hearts. It's like a flower without roots, once it's on it's own it will wither and die. Seeds need to be planted at an early age, and when the seeds begin to sprout and grow, all will see the results.

While the seeds are growing and adulthood is taking place in the form of moral values, acts of kindness, and knowing what's right and wrong, we don't always see the results of our teachings. But with time, the very things that have been planted will take root and blossom.

We have to rely on our faith that we have taught them well. Taught them to be themselves and not anyone else. We gave them life, but they have to live their own lives. In addition to giving them roots as parents, we have a great responsibility to provide a solid foundation for them to go forward.

We as parents are like the animal family. They give birth, teach their young to find food, fly, swim or whatever it is they need to do in order to survive on their own. They know that day is coming. We as parents know the day of departure is coming, as well.

In order for our young to live a life with purpose we must plant the seed. Then they will be able to go forth with their lives. During the planting stage of the seeds and roots, we are building character and self-motivation within. So with this in mind, if and when life hands them a curve they can take it and keep moving forward.

Life goes in the forward direction, not reverse. The only time one should look back is to see where they came from or where they went wrong. A sense of direction will allow our young people to have the ability to turn all of their dreams into reality and with that the value of life will have a more meaningful affect on them and those around them.

Even with a sense of direction one still might fall and stumble, but with perseverance they can still make it. By and large, it is not the big task that causes one to stumble. It is typically the little one on the way to the big one.

Once these core values are instilled in our children they will be able to fulfill their highest goals and dreams. This will allow them to soar to the highest mountain and dreams. This will indeed give their lives purpose.

The seeds of greatness are not planted for any other reason than to see them reach upward, just like a tree. We cannot always tell how high a tree will grow, but with fertilizer and nourishing it will become just what it was intended to become.

The Cracked Pot

No one has been, is, or will be perfect. Sometimes when we look back on our lives we see some errors that were made. If we could, we would turn back the hands of time and start over again. Because of this, there may be someone who thinks you are destined to fail, not have anything or become anything in life.

Sure, we all have made errors in judgment, but that does not mean we have to remain in a desolate position, or a phase of life where we are not comfortable. Only by accepting the past, can we alter or change our path. That decision is totally up to each individual. Each of us has our own flaws. We are all cracked pots in some form or another. When we share our flaws with others, we can help and encourage one another.

When we accept ourselves for who we are, then we can accept others in the same manner. We can see others' hurt and pain, we will then be able to help each other move forward. Coming to grips with where you are and moving forward is the beginning of healing.

The positive choices we make for ourselves will benefit us greatly. We are constantly evaluating and re-evaluating our choices on a daily basis. We should ask ourselves, "Is this right for me at this time?" In looking back, I could have gone in another direction, but I didn't. So this time I will evaluate my choices. By doing this we can move from the comfort zone of our lives and take advantage of the power of choice we have.

We must forge ahead in order to re-establish our self-esteem. Focus on the good and not the bad. Believe in yourself and you will be on the road to success. I had to work harder at being successful, but I made it. All you have to do is work on pleasing yourself and not anyone else.

Let's not be afraid to look at everything that has brought us to where we are in life, because there is always some good to be found if we look hard enough. I am convinced that our happiness or unhappiness in life depends greatly on how we view life. It all starts with a made up mind. Each new step will bring you closer to your goals.

One important secret in life is to refuse to allow temporary setbacks to defeat you. These are indeed temporary. You do not have to remain cracked or broken. You can look at every situation and say to it, "I am more than this," and then move ahead.

We all have something to share or do in life. That's why we cannot ever give up or quit on anything we want to do. We can allow our lives to impact others in such a way that it will be rewarding to all that we come in contact with.

The life we choose to live will be the life we live. If we choose a life based on our past we will be unhappy with life and ourselves, as well. This will help seal the cracks in the pot. We don't have to eat what's on our plate, we can go to the smorgasbord of life and this will change the very fabric of our lives. When we become flexible in life, then we will never again become bent out of shape. It's simply called moving ahead.

"You cannot erase the past. You must let it go.
You cannot change yesterday; you must accept the lessons learned."

(Author Unknown)

Finding Your Special Place

I believe that we are all destined to do something in life. We just need to find out what that something is. Ask yourself a valuable question. What is it that I want to do? Then make sure it is right for you and make certain that it is what you want for yourself. You have to find the path that's right for you. Research and read about your decision.

Education is the key that will unlock any door in any direction you choose to go in. We all have a purpose in life, but you must work on your goals and desires to move closer to your dream. It is important to note that not everyone is going to be a lawyer, doctor, teacher, or judge. Every profession is important. You might need to focus on one or two areas. If one does not work the other one will. The most important thing is to focus. The key is finding your purpose and being the best that you can be. It does not matter what it is, everyone's choice for themselves is important. Just be the best, because your self-worth is on the line.

This quote by Dr. Martin Luther King, Jr. sums up how you should look at your job, goals or opportunities: "No work is insignificant. All labor that uplifts humanity has dignity and importance and should be undertaken with a great deal of excellence."

Everything you lay your eyes on started in someone's mind. In order to be successful you must have a plan.

That's the difference between success and failure. If you don't have a plan you will fail. I have confidence in all of you that you will achieve your dreams and goals. When you have confidence in yourself, you can see yourself crossing the finish line of your dreams.

When you make decisions that will affect your life, you need to keep three people in mind: ME, MYSELF, AND I. Whatever decision you make will affect you first. There lies within each person a huge reservoir of untapped potential for achievement, success, happiness, health, and greater prosperity. You all have it on the inside. It's like a huge ocean unsailed, a new continent unexplored, a world of possibilities waiting to be released toward some great good, and only you know what that is.

My generation has passed the torch, now it is up to you all to take it and keep moving forward. Remember, the future belongs to you. So if you resolve in advance to persist until you succeed, then you will be successful at whatever you want to do in life. While talking about other great people, why not become one yourself?

Talk is cheap. Results and outcomes are the best measures of progress. We can talk all day long, but at the end of the day, our lives should show something positive. I want to see some positive results from you all.

You are already empowered with everything you need to go forth and become the person that you want to become. My question to you is, have you found your special place? That's a question only you can answer.

Achievement requires more than vision; it takes courage, resolve and tenacity. When you look in the mirror, always see yourself as the person you want to be. See yourself as strong, confident, and competent. The person you see is the person you will be.

Remember you are writing your tomorrows based on your accomplishments today. So make sure you see yourself crossing that finish line. You might want to know how I will see myself crossing that finish line. Think about it and visualize yourself crossing the line. Whatever you want to do in life, see yourself doing it. Do you see yourself? Imagine that you can be anything, be it an electrician, plumber, hair stylist, pilot, mechanic, factory worker, nurse, barber, or computer analyst.

You all are filled with so much knowledge and you have all of the resources available to you. Education is the key that will keep all of the doors open for you. Remember we all have made mistakes in life and my name is at the top of the list. But we all have choices. We can remain where we are or we can pick ourselves up and move forward.

Fear is not an option for me and it should not be for you, either. I have learned that fear has no power, unless we empower it by giving into it. Sometimes obstacles are the stepping stones to success. So instead of giving yourself reasons why you can't, give yourself reasons why you can. You must remember that we are standing on the shoulders of many great leaders who have proven that whatever you want can come to pass through hard work and persistence. Reap the harvest that you have labored for, because your success in life depends on the choices you make.

Finally, you are influenced by your associations. Who are you hanging out with? Can your friends help you get to the next level and beyond? If the answer is no, then it is time to think about changing friends.

Do not spend your time on voices that do not count. Allow your life to be an impact upon your friends and their lives should impact your life, as well. Remember: Opportunity plus Ability equals Accountability. Just believe in yourself, and no mountain will be too high. I believe in all of you and I know you will find your Special Place.

Lessons Learned

I'm my own person and this is a fact,
I follow my lead and I know how to act,
It took a long time to understand who I am
But I finally got the message it was a hard lesson learned.

If you believe in yourself and stay on the right track,
No one can make you have a bad setback,
Believe in yourself and as a matter of fact
Positive people and friends you will attract.

Lessons learned are things that happen in life,
You have to experience pain, heartbreak and other kinds of strife
To understand the true meaning of life,
To become stronger, better and more positive,
Use the information that others have to give.

Lessons learned are the act of living life.
Listening, assessing and considering advice,
to help you grow, learn and find a better way,
that's how to live the American way today.

Rose Jackson-Beavers

Articles to Encourage Your Mind

Creating the Audacity of Hope

What does audacity mean? It is defined in the dictionary as boldness.

After reading Senator Barack Obama's book, I think we all need audacity of hope. I challenge young people to not just talk about great people, why not reach up and get your share and become a great person? It is not just set aside for others; you have a share, as well.

Education will allow you to live your life with a great measure of dignity. Education is the key that will unlock any door in any direction you choose to go in. Education will give you the rite of passage and the spirit of hope, it helps you to have the audacity to believe in yourself. We cannot blame anyone but ourselves if we do not get to the place in our lives where we want to be.

Why is education so important, you ask? It is important because it is what is needed to become an expert in your field. It shows that you took all the necessary steps to learn your craft. Finally, it is because those who are in the power to employ you require it.

Our ancestor's went through a lot to assure that we could have an education. I challenge you as young people to not allow their efforts, struggles, and deaths to be in vain. Doors have been opened, victory has been won, and the doors are waiting for you to open them. Once you have that boldness, you will be able to see yourself crossing the finish line of your goals and dreams.

Be bold. Have that sense of strength and move toward your goals. The sacrifice you make in getting your education is immeasurable, when you measure it up against a lifetime. You are here to innovate, not to duplicate. Come up with new ideas, research new ways of finding cures.

Study to find a cure for incurable diseases, or for how older people can live longer. Find a cure for the common cold. I have a grandson who is Autistic. There is no cure, but if you all work hard and find a cure, then maybe other parents will not have to go through the pain of seeing their children with Autism.

Whatever direction you choose to go in, the doors are open. If you prepare for life with all your heart and passion, then you will overcome whatever gets in your way. If your dreams fall and break into 1,000 little pieces and you pick up just one and start over again, that will still put you one step closer to your goals. Remember, a million miles start with one step.

We all have struggles, but education is the strength for the struggle. You are already empowered with everything you need on the inside to make all of your dreams come true. God gave each of us a purpose in life. We will not all be teachers or pilots, but we are all destined to be great. It is our choice.

I ask you, and expect you, to be the best at whatever you do. Become all that you can be, and allow the person on the inside to be seen by others on the outside. It is the result that counts. A beautiful garden will be the result of your harvest. After all, results will show for themselves. If you do not try, you will not succeed. Opportunity will not come and knock on everybody's door, so you must be prepared to do the knocking. There are many doors out there, do not allow them to remain closed.

As I mentioned earlier, Senator Barack Obama, is truly standing on the shoulders of great leaders. He is running for President of the United States. There was a time when that was not possible.

Senator Obama is walking through doors that have been opened, but education was the stepping stone that allowed him to walk through those doors. So you see, education is the key that will and can unlock any door you choose.

Without education, he would not be where he is today. His first step was to graduate high school, then go on to college. He is a lawyer who became a senator and now a presidential candidate, and the rest is history. It all started with him making up his mind that education was very important in securing his future. He also believed in himself.

It's School Time Again

Returning to school after a long summer is sometimes hard to do. You've enjoyed the hot summer days and now it's time to refocus on your dreams and visions. It's time to ask yourself an all important question: Am I on the right track to finding the right career for me? Will I be happy with the choices I am about to make?

Our lives are shaped by our thoughts and actions. We are accountable for our actions as well as our reactions. It is up to us to use every advantage. We cannot blame anyone if we never try to obtain our goals.

We are empowered from within to succeed in whatever career we desire to be in. One thing to remember is to decide what's right before you decide what's possible. Empowerment is not "Giving Power to the People." No one can give you power, it has to start with you. Rather, it is showing and encouraging you to release the knowledge, desire, potentials, experience, and sense of one's self-motivation and pride you already have within.

Each of us have a talent within us to achieve success, but the key to success is having the ability to identify and develop our own particular talent. And that starts with us going deep within ourselves and figuring out what it is that we are created to do and become.

In doing so, you would have cultivated an unshakeable and unbreakable character within yourself. This will truly be the wind beneath your wings. Another thing to remember is that you cannot make progress without making decisions. Just remind yourself along the way that you have a tremendous reservoir of potential, and therefore you are quite capable of doing anything you set your mind to do.

Use your potential to become your dream. Our minds are like parachutes, they only function when they are open. The only thing that stands between a person and what he/she wants to do in life is the will to try and the faith to believe that it is possible. When you absolutely believe in your ability to succeed, nothing can stop you.

Everything is predicated on your belief in yourself and what you want to do. Remember, the future belongs to you. So if you resolve in advance to be persistent until you succeed, then you will be successful at whatever you want to do in life. Just say to yourself as Jesse Jackson quoted, "If my mind can conceive it, and my heart can believe it, then I know I can achieve it." The mind was created to learn and has a huge capacity to do so.

So, as you think of your dreams, goals, and visions for your future, begin today to take those very important steps to make them come alive. As Jim Rohn stated, "The miracle of the seed and soil is not available by affirmation, it is only available by labor."

When you maximize all of your potential, you can achieve your goals. There is so much potential in each and every one of you. There are no limitations on what you can become, have, or do, except the ones you place on yourself. We all have the ability to change our lives and our circumstances. We just need to know how to tap into the power we have within. Utilize those around you to realize your dreams. Work with your teachers, school counselors and pastors to find educational scholarships or to help put you on the right track to success.

There is no way to get around being challenged in life, but defeat is optional. That's a choice I hope you do not make. So how do you tap into this power? You look deep within yourself and decide what it is that you want in life, where you want to be.

You must think about and get rid of any conditions, associates, or problems that hold you back from achieving your goals. An example of this is when a young man went to a technical school in order to study computers because that was what he wanted to do. He figured out how to bridge the gap between where he was and where he wanted to be.

Now he is in upper management with the local phone company and he is writing computer programs for the company, as well. He didn't let anything hold him back. Though he did not attend college at that time, he went to technical school.

In order to be a goal achiever:
- Bridge the gap between where you are and where

you want to be.
- Bring your body, mind and spirit together. This will effectively help you to realize your dreams.
- Select and prioritize your goals in the most effective way.

Becoming empowered is something you must learn to do. Empowerment isn't magic. You must take some steps toward it and recognize that there could be some setbacks along the way. But with persistence and perseverance, changes can take place. Along the way to empowerment there is growth and maturity.

When you become empowered you are able to:
- Make decisions
- Take risks
- Be persistent
- Be responsible
- You have confidence
- You are not afraid

To become successful all you have to do is move yourself forward by taking one step at a time. Starting on the road to success is basically moving your feet one step at a time in the direction you want to go.

Let me share a conversation with you that I had with a young lady who was working at a Steak 'N Shake Restaurant. I asked her if she was in school and her reply was, "I am waiting for my GED test scores to come back in order for me to enroll in the University of Missouri and study Research Medicine, in order to find a cure for cancer." She went on to say, "That's why I did not graduate, because I have cancer." So as the story goes, she knew exactly what she wanted to do in life and she moved her feet in the right direction to get there.

Now, if you take this same approach, you will be one step closer to finding "Your Purpose Driven Life." All you have to do is make up your mind as to what you want out of life and how you are going to get there and then go for it.

Take this approach and have courage. When you have courage you are able to discover who you are and what you want to do. When you discover this, you can obtain knowledge by attending college or a technical school. Now you can feel inspired and continue to build your self-esteem and become successful. We all have a purpose in life. We just need to find out what that purpose is.
Let me share this with you:

Resolve says:

When you look at mountains many things go through your mind. It is too high. Boy, it's steep, or it is so rocky. But what if you have to climb it to get to where you are going? Would you be able to? Many have tried to climb mountains and some were successful and some died trying to get to the top. But many have climbed them, anyway. You know why? Because they wanted to try. So whatever it is you want out of life, do it. Just try. Then at least you can say you tried. You did your best. Success is waiting for you. !!!!!

Life Can Be Challenging

Life can be challenging at times. There is so much peer pressure around and for teenagers that is a major problem. My challenge to all students is to stay focused and be persistent with your studies. Without a strong degree of persistence you will not get that passing grade you want or need.

Do not give in to the challenges that you might face. By giving in, you will only have a lack of courage, low self-esteem, and no motivation to move forward to achieve that fulfilling future that you want for yourself. Your choices are the hinges of your destiny. With that in mind, you want more than a hinge for your future.

If you lose sight of your goals, no matter what grade level you are in, you will start a downward trend and that is not the direction you want to go. Believe it or not, there is a creative spirit within all of us, desiring to be free. Guess what? Doors are standing open and opportunities are waiting. Under no circumstances should you allow the challenges of life to alter your direction. Teachers, counselors, the library, and other resources are there for you.

Challenge yourself to greatness. After all, it is not set aside for others. Look up, reach out, and get your share. None of the above will happen if education is not the priority in your life. The key that you need to unlock those doors is education.

So in the words of Dr. Martin Luther King Jr.: "The ultimate measure of a person is not where he or she stands in moments of comfort and convenience, but where he stands at times of challenge and controversy." No matter what you face in life, never lose your desires, because they are the stimulant to keep you motivated to fulfill your dreams.

No matter what, the ongoing challenges of life will not abate or diminish, even while you are on you journey to your life's destination. Remember, no one can limit your growth but you yourself.

Sometimes, if homework seems very hard, stop, look, and listen to that person that is on the inside of you, telling you that you can do it. That person is you. Your future is being purchased daily by what you invest into it today. Believe in yourself as I believe in you.

Summer Challenge Part II

My challenge to all students during the summer is to read, because reading will allow you to be a couple of books ahead when it comes time to do book reports. With summer gone and the fall school year starting, why not continue to read? Why not challenge yourself? When others turn on the television or start to play games, why not go into the other room and read? If you commit to one hour of reading a day, just think about how many books you will be able to read. Books have a lot of hidden treasures that are contained on its pages.

Everything you do feeds your future. If you sow good seed now, then when it is harvest time, you will have an abundance of knowledge stored up for yourself. Remember, without action there is no harvest. You must have a good and positive attitude as to what it is you want out of life. "A positive thinker sees the invisible, feels the intangible, and achieves the impossible." (Author unknown) So when you think it is impossible to achieve your goals, just imagine the invisible. You might not be able to see it now, but if you work toward your destination you will see yourself crossing the finish line of your goals.

Why not be a risk taker and surprise yourself and see just how far you can really go. Since the future belongs to you, why not carve out the future that's right for you? And it all starts with you putting forth some extra efforts in order to do your best in school and get good grades.

Then you will be on your way to your destination and you will be able to see the invisible. If you believe in yourself then your faith will be the substance of things hoped for and the evidence of things not seen. So it is really up to you as far as your glass of life being half-empty or half-full. It all starts in your mind.

Why not continue to read and challenge yourself to get or stay at the top of your class? You will be helping the teacher help you when you do your best on your assignments.

For this school year, focus on the grades you want to have, not on what you did last year. Last year is gone and will not return. You are in the present, but your future is on the way. Continue to read and go beyond your expectations or your wildest dreams.

The challenge is still on!

Turning Stress into Success

It is a common knowledge that being stressed out prevents you from maximizing your potential. There is not much you can do when you are so stressed you cannot think. Stress will not only kill us, it also slows our bodies down. Therefore, it is important to seek ways to release the stress that your body is carrying around.

There are many ways that you can become successful. The first and most important step toward success is the feeling that you can and will succeed. You have to believe that it is not only the will to win, but you must have the will to prepare yourself to win and to beat all odds. I challenge you to get so wrapped up in homework, school projects, and making the best grade for this year that you will not focus on failure.

Think about this. To release stress you must accept the unchangeable. Everything that has happened is unchangeable. What you need to do is learn from your experiences.

We all have made errors in life. If we went to the left and realized it was not right, then we go to the right next time. How can you change the past when it is gone? It is history. Why not just learn from your experiences and move forward? In order to be successful during this part of the school year, set your goals and standards high.

Next, remember to change the things you can. What you

can change is how and why you did certain things in the past. For instance, if your choices got you into a jam, tell yourself, that will not happen again. Remember, you are going in a new direction now. You are now in control of your thoughts and actions. We do have control over our thought patterns. You are braver, stronger, and smarter than you think.

Finally, to release stress you must avoid the unacceptable. Do all you can to avoid bad behavior. Make changes whenever and wherever you can. Remember, time is of the essence at this time of the school year. "The time is always right to do what is right," stated Dr. Martin Luther King Jr. So put that extra effort into doing your homework, because extra credits are always in order. There is a point in your life that you must reach. That point is your destiny. Make sure you are doing the right things in order to stay focused in order to get there.

Not that you have accepted the unchangeable and are in the process of changing the changeable, and avoiding the unacceptable, welcome difficulties and obstacles as valuable steps on the ladder to success. The doors to success sometimes swing on the hinges of obstacles.

There are two things that make people afraid. They are knowledge and taking action. Most people are afraid to seek knowledge for fear that they will have no more excuses for not achieving all that is possible. Others just don't have the courage to try to further their education. There is no failure in trying. Release this fear. I believe that each person has far more intelligence than he or she has ever used.

Most people refuse to take action. They take exception to blaming others. I can't do it, because that is not the right attitude to have to move forward. Taking action will only move you closer to your goal. Stop making up excuses and move forward with steam. Without having stress, I believe the greatest achievement of your life is ahead of you. Release the stress and move forward.

Attitude

Now that school is well on its way, what are your choices for this school year? It all starts with a good positive attitude. So I challenge students to think positive. After all, circumstances will arrive and get you off track. Thinking positive will give you the upper hand.

You have goals and dreams and it takes persistence to bring them to completion. The success of goals begins with a made up mind to move forward. Henry W. Longfellow said, "Perseverance is a great element of success." Once you start on the road, you have to be persistent at all times.

Ask yourself, "What am I willing to give up for the attainment of my goals?" You have all of the reasons to achieve your greatest dreams. Because, after all, the path you want to take will lead you to the goals set aside for you. Whatever your destination is, education will be beneficial to you in getting there.

The only limit to your realization of your tomorrow is when you allow doubt to creep in today. When you have a strong, good and positive attitude about attending class everyday and doing your very best on your homework that will allow you to discover things about yourself that you never really knew. That will allow the instruments of your mind to stretch and go beyond the norm.

Look at how candles cannot burn until you light them.

Education will give you the flame that you need to become all you dream to be. You are already empowered with everything you need to see you through, just press forward and see your dreams become realized.

The school year is well on its way, so hang in there with every fiber of persistence you can muster. The end results depend on one person.... you! Everyday, tell yourself that you are ready for the New Year. Tell yourself to follow through on your ideas and continue to work hard toward your success. Make good choices, it's all about the power of your attitude. That will allow you to take the leadership position within your circle. Learn to express, not impress. Strive to make a difference in your life and then allow that difference to impact others.

New journeys await you. Allow your choices for this school year to take you to the summit of your goals. After all, the heart of education is the education of one's heart. Do not allow what's on the inside to remain there.

Something to Think About

With all of the tragedies that are happening, I look around and see people who have problems much greater than mine. Yet, they confront life with a courageous and honest determination within themselves. It makes me stop and realize how small my worries are in comparison and how I should try that much harder to be happy, tolerant, understanding and caring toward others. It encourages me to believe in my own abilities, but most of all to be thankful for all I have everyday of my life.

I have learned that, at any given moment, a smile can change one's direction, and who is to know when a smile is needed by someone else. Nothing is worth more than this day, because tomorrow is not promised to anyone.

Learning Has Purpose

I challenge all students to develop a purpose for learning. That purpose should be to increase your level of self-esteem and to prepare you for all of the opportunities that are waiting for you. The pathway to success is through education. Without educational knowledge, one's dreams will not come to fruition.

On your way to becoming that successful person that you want to be you might run into a stumbling block along the way, but just remember, if one's dreams fall and break into a 1000 little pieces, never be afraid to pick up just one of them and begin again. A quote by Michael Jordan says, "Step by step, I can't think of any other way of accomplishing anything." You know he took a lot of steps on the court and he made it to the top of his goals and dreams.

Since this is a new year, why not have a new prospective on your school assignments? Take those extra steps. Education is not simply the process of gathering knowledge, but also learning how to analyze that knowledge and apply it in a more practical sense. Without the educational skills and abilities that you will gain from doing your very best in school, you would be at a disadvantage that you do not want for yourself.

Education and knowledge is power. It doesn't give power; it energizes potential, which will allow you to move down the pathway to success. Along the way, be curious. For knowledge will not acquire you, you have to acquire it. Start by doing what's necessary, then what's possible, and suddenly you will find yourself doing the impossible. There are many resources available through your school, teachers, counselors, librarians and, most of all, your parents. With so many avenues available it is hard to miss out on getting the best grades you can.

Always bear in mind that your own resolution to succeed is more important than anything else. So on that thought, it is time to prioritize in order to make this school year the most successful one yet. And that will be the catalyst for each year after, until you reach your goals and potentials.

Within you right now is the power to do things you never dreamed possible. This power becomes available to you as soon as you decide, "This is going to be a better year for me. I will put forth my very best." With elevated thoughts, you will begin to act and believe that it is impossible to fail. By having a different perspective you can read more, prepare yourself for the next book report, take courses that will prepare you for college, and visualize yourself in the capacity where you want to be in life.

There is a great purpose in learning. It is a great investment into one's life. Success seems to be largely a matter of hanging on after others have let go.

Every Success Starts With a Plan

A plan needs direction. Success is nothing more than a few simple disciplines, practiced everyday. The purpose of life is more than just being happy. The main purpose is to matter, to be productive, and to make a difference in someone else's life.

What are your plans for the rest of the school year? If you plan to finish this year with good grades, then it is high time to put your plan in place. I like what Aristotle said when he stated, "The roots of education may be bitter sometimes, but the fruit is sweet." I know that getting up every morning and going to class to sit and listen is hard. But the rewards of being an educated person are so sweet. If you want to have the things in life that make living pleasurable you have to make some positive choices about your education. Truly your choices do have consequences. So do not get caught up trying to please others and forget about what is important to you.

I don't know the key to your success because we all have different keys. One thing I do know is that the key to failure is to try to please everyone else. Just make sure you have the key that is right for you. Go ahead and study hard in order to bring your dreams to life. If you do not do this for yourself, no one else is going to. The real winners in life are the ones who look at every situation with an expectation that they can make it work or make it better.

With your vision for yourself in mind, figure out what it is that you need to do in order to have that fulfillment that you want for yourself. Now is the time to put in place everything you need in order to see yourself at the place in life you want to be. A mind is a terrible thing to waste. It is like a parachute, in that it does not work unless it is open.

Don't worry about possible mistakes along the way. The person who has never made mistakes has never tried anything new. Another thing to keep in mind is, ordinary riches can be stolen, but the richness of education cannot. The richness gained through education is the one precious thing that cannot be taken from you. It is yours for a lifetime.

Do not allow anyone to tell you that you cannot become whatever or whomever you want to be. You will only hit what you aim for, so my challenge to you is to aim high, as high as you can. Setting a goal is not the only thing that is required; it is deciding how you will go about achieving it and staying with your plan. Remember, every successful story started with a plan.

Intellectual Growth

This school year is almost over. I challenge every student to put forth your best. You want to leave this school year with flying colors. When test time comes give it all you have. Do not take anything for granted, study and prepare for those final days of the school year. Even if you are on the right track and you think you have it all together, it will benefit you if you put forth that extra effort.

Just remember you are responsible and accountable for the grades you receive. Doing the best that you can at this time puts you in the best position for those last days of school. Your results will be the time you put in preparing and dedication to ending this year on a high note. Do not just say, "I am doing my best." You have got to succeed in doing what is necessary.

Intellectual growth should commence at birth and cease only at death. Learning should be and is a lifelong mission. Our lives begin to end the day we become silent about things that matter. When we carve out a niche for ourselves, we should not be happy until we receive it, no matter how long it takes.

It all starts now, today. Where you are now will direct your future. The choices are yours. How much time have you dedicated to what you want to do in life? How different will your life be when you really know what is deeply important to you? Keep that in mind and you will be able to manage thoughts each day, to do and be what really matters most. Follow your heart and use your intuition to get where you want to go.

I challenge you to not be afraid. Wrap yourself in obtaining your goals and desires and achieve your dreams and you will not be afraid. Then you will be able to say, imagine this, imagine me. I succeeded.

Each of you are beautiful people. You are like the butterfly that will eventually come out of its cocoon and unfurl his wings to soar. You must get off the ground and learn to ride with the breeze, smell the flowers and let your beauty show. This will allow your intellectual growth to come forth.

Food For Thought

I challenge all students to challenge yourselves. Challenges are tools you can use for yourself to get through all of the assignments that are on your plate. Food for thought: If you have confidence in yourself, then you are on your way to accomplishing what you set out to do. Your main task in life is to give birth to the person that dwells deep within, in order to become the person on the outside that you want to be.

Food for thought: Look back at your accomplishments and see what you have accomplished (the positive not the negative) to this point. Tell yourself, "I am powerful beyond all measure." And since you are at this time of the school year, the balance of this year will even be greater than before. Think about this, Losers make promises they do not keep, many are broken. Winners are more committed and continue to work on their goals. From this point on release your fears, re-kindle your purpose and embrace the challenges in your life.

Food for thought: One's mind, once strengthened by new ideas, new visions and aspirations, never regains its original dimensions. Once you act on one idea you will be compelled to go on to the next. Always be curious, because knowledge does not or will not seek you, you must put forth the effort for yourself. And before you know it you will be doing the impossible.

Food for thought: Since education is the key that will

unlock any door in any direction you choose to go in, watch your manner of speech, dwell on the positive not the negative. Once this change has taken place, your days will be more peaceful and confirming. Your attitude determines your altitude.

With the above being said, keep the school year in focus. Hold yourself responsible and to a higher standard than anyone expects of you, even yourself. Morals, values, and attitude are the fundamental ingredients to success.

Tips for Becoming Successful

Tip 1

Dressing for Success: First impression is the only thing that people know about you when they have no real experiences or information about your work, your behavior or your attitude. People judge you by your cover until they get to know you. Only then can they look at what is inside. Your appearance is the first thing that people see. Always dress appropriately, with clean clothes and keep your body parts covered. The only place that sagging pants are acceptable is in prison. Don't lose out on an opportunity because you want to wear pants down to your knees.

Tip 2

Sacrifices:
The sacrifices you are making or are about to make are immeasurable when you measure them up against a lifetime, because the goals you are aiming for will be yours for a lifetime. After all, it is by spending oneself, that one becomes rich.

Tip 3

Don't Take the Easy Road:
Take more than the basic classes in high school. Not only will this increase your grade point average, but it will show college recruiters that you did not take the easy route. This will prepare you for the next level once you get to college. College classes are more detailed and demanding than high school. Taking the easy road will cause unnecessary struggling in your college courses.

Tip 4

Self-Direction:
Take time to figure out what direction you are headed in. You have choices in life. Choose the ones that are right for you. Then you will be able to see yourself crossing the finish line of your goals and dreams. Just remember that yesterday's passion may or may not serve tomorrow's goals!

Tip 5

Not Enough Accountability:
You are accountable for the grades and courses you take. Your senior year should not be a year of partying and having

fun. If you take this approach you will find yourself behind in the basic studies when you arrive at college. Challenge yourself to do the opposite, by applying yourself as much as possible, because you will benefit first and foremost.

Tip 6

Waiting Too Late to Start Planning for College:
It's never too early to start preparing and planning for your future. By the time you are in middle school you should have an idea of what you want to do and know the direction you need to go in. Now if you wait until your junior and senior year, that's too late, not that you can't do it, but so much time has been lost. More of the basic classes and even college level classes should have been taken by this time.

Tip 7

What about Your G.P.A.?
Your grade point average is very crucial at this time. Colleges not only look at your GPA, but what courses were taken. A good grade in English is fine, but what about Math, Calculus, Biology, etc.? Be very careful about the courses you take, go a couple of steps farther.

Remember, your choices do have consequences.

Tip 8

Ask for Help if Needed:
If you need help, ask. Teachers, counselors, parents, and administrators all are there to help you make the right decisions and to help you choose the right direction you need to go in. After all, when old patterns are broken, new worlds emerge. Your self-image and habits tend to go together. Once you make up your mind to change one area you will automatically change the other.

Notes

Notes

Notes

Notes

Notes

Notes

Notes

Notes

Notes

About the Author

Speaker, Education Columnist and Author

Lydia M. Douglas is a Motivational Speaker/Author with a desire to help others realize that they all have a well of untapped resources, unfulfilled dreams, and desires within. She is retired from her job of 26 years. She resides in St. Louis, Missouri. She is a Columnist for the Spanish Lake Word newspaper in St. Louis, MO. Lydia has spoken at more than 20 schools throughout the Metropolitan area and is well received by the students in the classes.

Lydia's Publications

Stepping Stones to Success is a collection of essays that will reveal new paths and directions to motivate and inspire the readers to reach their highest goals.

Taking Care of Business asks the question "Is your family prepared to handle your estate once you depart from this world." Have you mapped out your preferred funeral and burial plans?

Reaching Higher Heights is outlines effective strategies and goals to help students accomplish their dreams. Relevant to students of all ages!

To request information regarding presentations or to order books e-mail me at: **Lydia@BooksByLydia.Com**. She is also available for student workshops.

Phone: 314-741-2532 or 314-608-9279

www.ingramcontent.com/pod-product-compliance
Lightning Source LLC
Chambersburg PA
CBHW020015050426
42450CB00005B/490